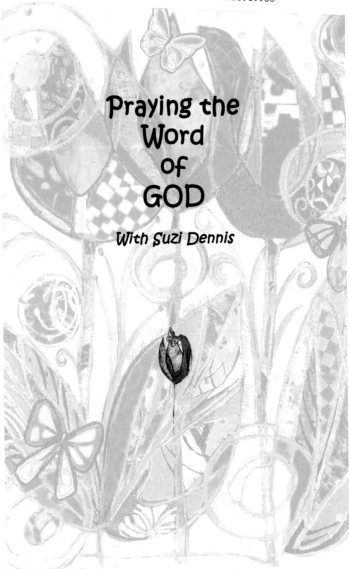

Praying the
Word
of
GOD

With Suzi Dennis

DEDICATION

To my daughter Shari,
who on March 11, 2013
walked through the door
from this life to eternal life
with Jesus.
Her leaving took me
to a deeper place of prayer
than I had ever been.
For my son Mark who I love dearly
and for my husband John
who is my helpmate and my hero.

"But when you pray, go into your room
and shut the door and pray to your
Father who is in secret. And your
Father who sees in secret will reward
you."
Matthew 6:6

Introduction

Several years ago I heard it said, "If you are trying to make a decision and don't know what to do, go to the scriptures", so I did. And what I found out was that if I am seeking the scriptures for answers, then that is how I need to pray. So, being a journaler most of my life, I started keeping a journal of these prayers and I turn to it daily still today.

I am foremost an artist and have created many works of art over the years inspired by the Holy Scriptures. On March 11, 2013 my life changed forever when my daughter Shari went to Heaven. I turned again to the scriptures, the Word of God, and prayer to strengthen me and help me through this journey.

In 2015 I decided to start a daily facebook page of praying back the Word of God and have posted a daily scripture and prayer since January 19, 2015 and continue to as of the publication of this book. Praying this way has greatly strengthened my prayer life and I wanted to pass some of these prayers to others along with art I have created, inspired by these scriptures.

I invite you into this Sanctuary of Prayer.

My prayer is that you will find strength in these prayers and learn to go to the scriptures and seek guidance as you learn, on your own, to pray back the Word of God.

Blessings,
Suzi

"And he who was seated
on the throne said,
"Behold, I am making all things new."
Also he said,
"Write this down,
for these words are
trustworthy and true."
Revelation 21:5

Pray Back Revelation 21:5
Oh the promise straight from You
Father!! You are making everything new
for us who believe in Your Son Jesus!!
You have written it down and it is
trustworthy and true!!
Thanks be to God!
Amen and Amen!

"Sing praises to the LORD,
O you his saints,
and give thanks to his holy name.
For his anger is but for a moment,
and his favor is for a lifetime.
Weeping may tarry for the night,
but joy comes with the morning."
Psalm 30:4-5

Pray Back Psalm 30: 4-5

I sing praises to You Lord
and give You thanks
in remembrance for all
You have done for me.
I praise Your Holy Name .
You were angry at me
for only a moment,
but You will lavish
Your goodness on me
for a lifetime.
I may weep for a night,
but joy lifts me up
with the morning.
Amen

"And so, from the day we heard,
we have not ceased to pray for you,
asking that you may be filled with
the knowledge of his will in all
spiritual wisdom and understanding."
Colossans 1:9

Pray Back Colossans 1:9
Thank you Father, for the names
you whisper in my ear to pray for.
Each time You send me their name,
I pray and I won't stop praying
for them.I pray as they battle
life's struggles,diseases,
trials and temptations
that You will fill them with
the knowledge of
Your will for them
and send Your Spirit
to give them all the wisdom
and understanding
that is theirs to have.
Amen

"For whatever was written in former days was written for our instruction, that through endurance and through the encouragement of the Scriptures we might have hope. May the God of endurance and encouragement grant you to live in such harmony with one another, in accord with Christ Jesus, that together you may with one voice glorify the God and Father of our Lord Jesus Christ."
Romans 15:4-6

Pray Back Romans 15:4-6

Lord, I thank You for Your Holy Word which was written in the past to teach me. Words that through endurance and encouragement, give me hope. Now God I pray that You, the God who gives endurance and encouragement, will give me a spirit of oneness with my brothers and sisters in Christ, so that together, with one heart and mouth, we may glorify You, the Father of our Lord Jesus Christ. Amen

"Do not be deceived:
God is not mocked, for
whatever one sows, that
will he also reap. For the
one who sows to his own
flesh will from the flesh
reap corruption, but the
one who sows to the Spirit
will from the Spirit reap
eternal life."
Galatians 6:7-8

Pray Back Galatians 6:7-8

Father I pray to not be deceived
and know that You are
never to be mocked.
I know full well that whatever I do
to please MY selfish desires
will only bring trouble to my door,
but the things I do
to please Your Spirit Lord,
will bring to me eternal life
that only Your Spirit can give.
Amen

"For we do not wrestle against
flesh and blood, but against the
rulers, against the authorities,
against the cosmic powers over
this present darkness, against
the spiritual forces of evil in the
heavenly places. Therefore take
up the whole armor of God, that
you may be able to withstand
in the evil day, and having done all,
to stand firm."
Ephesians 6:12-13

Pray Back Ephesians 6:12-13

As I go through my day Lord, remind me what
your Word says about these earthly battles I
fight;that I do not struggle against man
but against the powers of darkness that rule
this dark world I live in;those authorities and
spiritual forces of evil that are in the
heavenly places. So today and every day,
I put on Your armor, all of it, so that
I will be ready for evil when it comes
my way and that I will be able to stand.
Amen

"Trust in the Lord with
all of your heart
and do not lean
on your own understanding.
In all your ways acknowledge Him
and He will make straight your paths."
Proverbs 3:5-6

Pray back Proverbs 3: 5-6
My Father God in Heaven,
I trust You with all that I am
and all that I have in me.
I don't pretend to
understand this life
and this world
and I'm not depending
on what I do understand.
You are most Holy,
You are God,
You are the "I Am"
and to You I turn
to find my way,
my path.
Amen

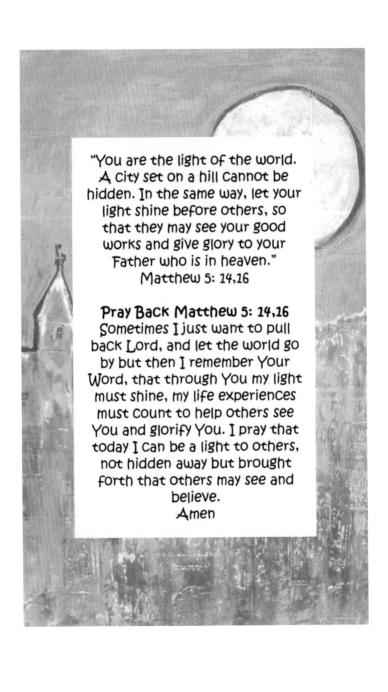

"You are the light of the world. A city set on a hill cannot be hidden. In the same way, let your light shine before others, so that they may see your good works and give glory to your Father who is in heaven."
Matthew 5: 14,16

Pray Back Matthew 5: 14,16
Sometimes I just want to pull back Lord, and let the world go by but then I remember Your Word, that through You my light must shine, my life experiences must count to help others see You and glorify You. I pray that today I can be a light to others, not hidden away but brought forth that others may see and believe.
Amen

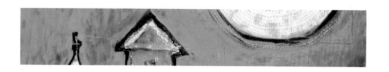

"Sing praises to the LORD,
O you his saints,
and give thanks to his holy name.
For his anger is but for a moment,
and his favor is for a lifetime.
Weeping may tarry for the night,
but joy comes with the morning."
Psalm 30:4-5

Pray Back Psalm 30:4-5
I sing praise to you My Lord along
with all Your saints and I give thanks
to You as I remember Your Holy Name
and remember that Your Name is holy.
I give thanks that when You are angry
with me it is only for a little while
knowing that You favor me forever.
Sorrow and sadness will come my way
but because I know You, it is
only here for a period of time
and then....the joy of a new day!
Thank you Father for Your
great mercies.
Amen

"But no human being can tame the tongue.
It is a restless evil, full of deadly poison.
With it we bless our Lord and Father,
and with it we curse people
who are made in the likeness of God.
From the same mouth
come blessing and cursing. My brothers,
these things ought not to be so."
James 3:8-10

Pray back James 3:8-10
How can I curse man and bless You
from the same mouth Lord?
But I do it...I can't seem to tame it
and sometimes I do it all at the
same time! Help me to remember
that man is made in Your image
and this should not be something
I do. I am learning Lord,
please continue to teach me
through Your Word.
Amen

"For you, O Lord, are good and forgiving
abounding in steadfast love
to all who call upon you.
Give ear, O LORD, to my prayer;
listen to my plea for grace.
In the day of my trouble
I call upon you,
for you answer me."
Psalm 86:5-7

Pray Back Psalm 86:5-7
What a forgiving and good God
You are Father! You have so much
love to all of us who call on You!
Please hear this prayer I pray
to You Lord, please hear my
distressed cry to You for mercy.
I call on You every day because
I know You will answer me.
Amen

"But I will sing of your strength;
I will sing aloud of your
steadfast love in the morning.
For you have been to me a fortress
and a refuge in the day of my distress."
Psalm 59:16

Pray Back Psalm 59:16

Each morning Lord, before I start
my day, I lift up my heart in prayer
to You and I marvel at Your power
and strength and Your eternal
love for me. You have been
my protection, my place of peace
and strength every day of my life and
even more so in the times of distress,
heartache and fear. I know that
no matter what, You are covering me
with Your strength. Thank You
Father, for Your great love.
Amen

"The LORD bless you and keep you;
The LORD make His face shine upon you,
And be gracious to you;
The LORD lift up His countenance upon you,
And give you peace.'"
Numbers 6:24-26

Pray Back Numbers 6:24-26
As I start my day Lord I hear
the echoes of the past bringing me
this blessing from You,
knowing that with each step I take
You will bless me and keep me safe.
That the shining light of Your Glory
will shine on me and that you will
give me peace in each situation
that comes in my path today.
Thank you Father, for being with me.
Amen

"walk in a manner
worthy of the calling
to which you have been called,
with all humility and gentleness,
with patience, bearing with
one another in love."
Ephesians 4:1-2

Pray back Ephesians 4:1-2
To be completely humble
and gentle and patient
is not an easy task for me Lord.
But Your Word says this is what
I am to do so I pray that You will
bear with me in love as I bear
with others in love and teach me
to be humble, gentle and patient.
Amen

"In my Father's house are many rooms.
If it were not so, would I have told
you that I go to prepare a place for you?
And if I go and prepare a place for you,
I will come again and will take you to myself,
that where I am you may be also."
John 14:2-3

Pray Back John 14:2-3

How blessed I am Lord, that
You have prepared a home
for me in heaven with You!
And You have promised me,
that when that place is ready,
You will come again to this earth
and take me there and I will
be with You forever and ever.
Thank You Jesus.
Amen

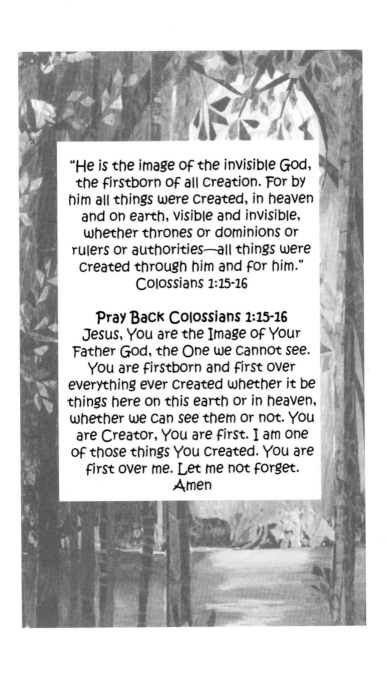

"He is the image of the invisible God, the firstborn of all creation. For by him all things were created, in heaven and on earth, visible and invisible, whether thrones or dominions or rulers or authorities—all things were created through him and for him."
Colossians 1:15-16

Pray Back Colossians 1:15-16
Jesus, You are the Image of Your Father God, the One we cannot see. You are firstborn and first over everything ever created whether it be things here on this earth or in heaven, whether we can see them or not. You are Creator, You are first. I am one of those things You created. You are first over me. Let me not forget.
Amen

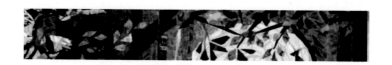

"And I will ask the Father,
and he will give you another Helper,
to be with you forever,
even the Spirit of truth,
whom the world cannot receive,
because it neither sees him
nor knows him.
You know him, for he dwells
with you and will be in you."
John 14:16-17

Pray Back John 14:16-17

Thank You Jesus for interceding
for me, for speaking to Your Father
and requesting a Helper for me,
One that will be with me forever,
The Holy Spirit, the Spirit of Truth.
I am so thankful I have received Him
and I know Him. It is through
knowing You, loving You and believing
in You that He dwells in me.
The world does not know Him,
but I do.
Amen

"But you, O LORD, are a shield about me,
my glory, and the lifter of my head.
I cried aloud to the LORD,
and he answered me
from his holy hill."
Psalm 3:3-4

Pray Back Psalm 3: 3-4

You are all around me Lord,
everyday and in every way.
You are here because
I have asked You to be here.
I have invited You into my Life.
You protect me, not from all
bad things happening,
but You protect me
when they do happen.
You are my glory and
You raise me up
when I am down.
When I cry out to You,
You hear me and
from on high You answer.
Praise be to You O Father.
Amen

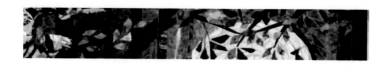

"Be still before the LORD
and wait patiently for him;
fret not yourself over the one
who prospers in his way,
over the man who carries out evil devices!
Refrain from anger, and forsake wrath!
Fret not yourself; it tends only to evil.
For the evildoers shall be cut off,
but those who wait for the LORD
shall inherit the land."
Psalm 37:7-9

Pray back Psalm 37:7-9
I will be still before You Lord
and listen and wait patiently.
I do not need to worry about
the success of others
who succeed through evil
and wicked ways.
I will turn away from anger
toward them because it only
hurts me. You will take care
of them. As for me, I will put
my hope in You and that is
my success.
Amen

"Hear, O Israel: The LORD our God,
the LORD is one.
You shall love the LORD your God
with all your heart and with all your soul
and with all your might."
Deuteronomy 6: 4-5

Pray Back Deuteronomy 6:4-5
This Shema You gave to Your people Israel
many years before you sent Your Son.
But then He came and told us the same thing.
How Important I have come to understand
God, that I am to love You and only You
with all I am and all I have. It's a command,
not a suggestion, from You my Father.
Help me never to fear impressing
this love on my family and my friends
and all who will hear me. Thank You Father.
Amen

"For the time is coming when people will not endure sound teaching, but having itching ears they will accumulate for themselves teachers to suit their own passions, and will turn away from listening to the truth and wander off into myths."
2 Timothy 4: 3-4

Pray Back 2 Timothy 4: 3-4
A time is coming and is already here. People in this world are turning to teaching that is not Yours Lord. They reach out to those who tell them what they want to hear, to what will keep them from the truth. I pray for them Father and give thanks that You turned me toward the truth of Your Word.
Amen

"But, as it is written,
"What no eye has seen,
nor ear heard,
nor the heart of man
imagined,
what God has prepared
for those who love him"
1 Corinthians 2:9

Pray Back 1 Corinthians 2:9
It is written in Your Word Lord!
What You have prepared for us in
life eternal with You, no one has seen
or heard about. No one's heart can even
imagine it. It fills my heart with joy
at the peace that awaits me there.
Thank You for this provision!
Amen

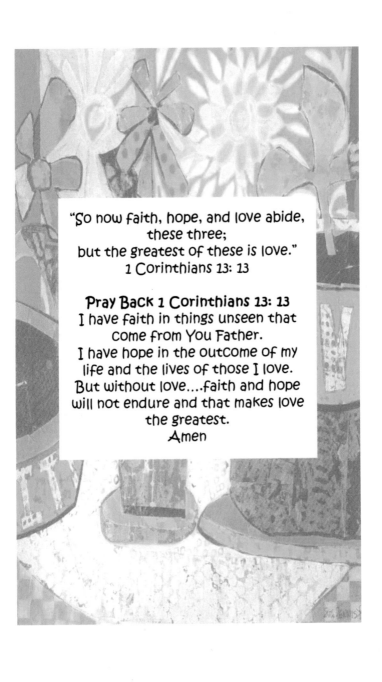

"So now faith, hope, and love abide,
these three;
but the greatest of these is love."
1 Corinthians 13: 13

Pray Back 1 Corinthians 13: 13
I have faith in things unseen that
come from You Father.
I have hope in the outcome of my
life and the lives of those I love.
But without love....faith and hope
will not endure and that makes love
the greatest.
Amen

"And he sat down and
called the twelve.
And he said to them,
"If anyone would
be first, he must be
last of all and
servant of all."
Mark 9:35

Pray Back Mark 9:35
This is a "me first" world we
live in Lord and You know that.
It is all around us every day,
that desire to rise above.
But that is not Your Word.
When I am feeling I'm not on top,
feeling inadequate, help me to
remember Your Words.
If I want to be first, I must be
last and serve others.
In Your Name Jesus, I pray.
Amen

"I love the LORD,
because he has heard
my voice and my pleas
for mercy. Because he
inclined his ear to me,
therefore I will call on him
as long as I live."
Psalm 116:1-2

Pray Back Psalm 116:1-2
Lord I love You!
Thank you for
not only hearing me but
for listening to my pleas
for mercy. Please know
Father, that I will always
call to You for the rest
of my life because I know
You listen.
Thank You Father.
Amen

"O you who
love the LORD,
hate evil!
He preserves the lives
of his saints;
he delivers them
from the hand
of the wicked."
Psalm 97:10

Pray Back Psalm 97:10

You are my Protector Father
and I love You and I do hate evil.
I hate what it is doing to this
world and the people in it.
But I thank You that I am
preserved and protected from
this evil and that I have You
in my life to deliver me from
the hand of the wicked.
Thank You Father.
Amen

"But he said to me,
"My grace is sufficient for you,
for my power is made perfect in
weakness." Therefore I will boast
all the more gladly of my weaknesses,
so that the power of Christ
may rest upon me."
2 Corinthians 12:9

Pray Back 2 Corinthians 12:9
It is so hard Lord, to be glad
for my weaknesses, but when
I read Your Word,
I understand why.
When I am weak Your grace
pours out on me and
Your power is then made
perfect and others see
Christ through my weakness.
It's not about me....
it's about You Lord.
Amen

"No temptation has overtaken
you that is not common to man.
God is faithful, and he will not
let you be tempted beyond
your ability, but with the
temptation he will also provide
the way of escape, that you may
be able to endure it."
1 Corinthians 10:13

Pray Back 1 Corinthians 10:13
Temptation is everywhere I go,
every day and You have said Lord
that these are common temptations
to all mankind and that you will not
allow temptations in my path beyond
my ability to bear them. Most of all Father,
You are faithful to show me a way out,
a different path. I rest knowing You
are always there if I will just look.
Amen

"Out of my distress
I called on the LORD;
the LORD answered me
and set me free.
The LORD is on my side;
I will not fear.
What can man do to me?"
Psalm 118:5-6

Praying back Psalm 118:5-6
I am hard pressed Lord
and I cry to You. You bring
me into a spacious place
of peace. You are with me Lord,
I will not be afraid.
What can man do to me?
Amen

"Be still, and know that I am God;
I will be exalted among the nations,
I will be exalted in the earth."
Psalm 46:10

Pray Back Psalm 46:10

To be still is one of the greatest
challenges in my life Lord,
but when I do, when I am still
and focus on knowing
YOU are GOD,
I am overwhelmed and
Graced with Your presence.
I exalt You Father in all the earth!
Amen

"And the glory of the LORD shall be revealed,
and all flesh shall see it together,
for the mouth of the LORD
has spoken."
Isaiah 40:5

Pray Back Isaiah 40:5
Your glory Lord is revealed everyday for all to see if we will only open our eyes and our ears. And one day Your glory will be revealed for all to see whose eyes and ears have been closed. Blessed be Your Name!
Amen

"Finally, brothers, whatever is true,
whatever is honorable, whatever is just,
whatever is pure, whatever is lovely,
whatever is commendable, if there is any
excellence, if there is anything
worthy of praise,
think about these things."
Philippians 4:8

Pray back Philippians 4:8
When I open my mouth to speak Lord,
when I sit down to meditate on
Your Word, when thoughts run amok
through my mind, remind me to honor
whatever is true, whatever is honorable,
whatever is just, whatever is pure,
whatever is lovely and whatever
is commendable. Teach me to turn
from impure thoughts and words
to what is excellent or praiseworthy
in Your sight.
Amen

"I love you, O LORD, my strength.
The LORD is my rock and my
fortress and my deliverer, my God,
my rock, in whom I take refuge,
my shield, and the horn of
my salvation,
my stronghold."
Psalm 18:1-2

Pray Back Psalm 18:1-2
Oh how I love you Lord.
I could not exist day to day
in this world without your strength.
To turn my ears to you each morning
and know you fortify and deliver me
gives me strength. And as the day
progresses and temptations cross my path
I feel the shield of your protection
going in front of me and the rock of
Your salvation underneath my feet.
You are my stronghold and without you,
I am nothing.
Amen

"Create in me a clean heart,
O God, and renew a right spirit
within me. Cast me not away from
your presence, and take not your
Holy Spirit from me. Restore to me
the joy of your salvation,
and uphold me with a willing spirit."
Psalm 51:10-12

Pray back Psalm 51:10-12

When the waters of my soul get
muddy Lord, I pray to You for a heart
that is clean and a right spirit to live
inside of me. And please never put me
to the side, away from Your presence
or take away Your Holy Spirit from me!
I need the joy of salvation in You
to sustain me through the day and
through life and a willing spirit to
receive these blessings.
Thank you Father.
Amen

\

"For God so loved the world,
that he gave his only Son,
that whoever believes in him
should not perish but have
eternal life.
John 3:16

Pray Back John 3:16
Look how much You love me Lord....
You sacrificed Your one and only
Son for me! In doing this You said
that If I believe in Him I will not die!
I will have life eternal with Him
and with You.
Thank You Abba Father,
for loving me that much.
Amen

"We ought always to give thanks
to God for you, brothers, as is right,
because your faith is growing abundantly,
and the love of every one of you for
one another is increasing.."
2 Thess. 1:3

Pray Back 2 Thess. 1:3
I thank You Father for my
Brothers and Sisters in Christ.
Because of their faith that is
growing more all the time,
the love they have for each other,
the love they have for me and
the love I have for them grows more
and more each day. They have been
so faithful to come along side of me.
May I always return it back to them.
Amen

"...who gives life to the dead
and calls into existence
the things that do not exist.
Romans 4:17

Pray Back Romans 4:17
I pray Father, for the things
in life that by a mere blink
of an eye, You can call into existence.
I thank You ahead of time and
give You praise for these things
I know are coming to pass
because You have the power.
Amen

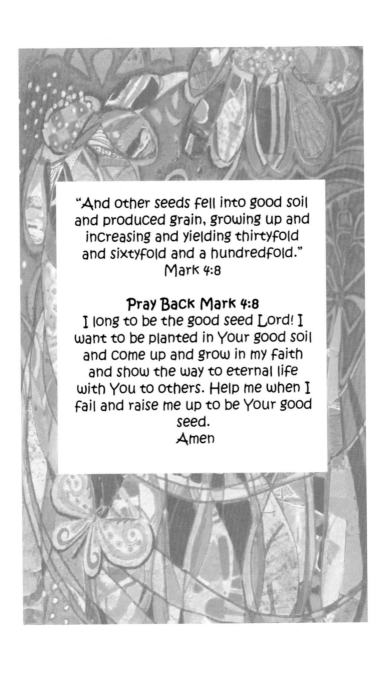

"And other seeds fell into good soil and produced grain, growing up and increasing and yielding thirtyfold and sixtyfold and a hundredfold."
Mark 4:8

Pray Back Mark 4:8
I long to be the good seed Lord! I want to be planted in Your good soil and come up and grow in my faith and show the way to eternal life with You to others. Help me when I fail and raise me up to be Your good seed.
Amen

"A new commandment I give to you,
that you love one another: just as
I have loved you, you also are to
love one another. By this all people
will know that you are my disciples,
if you have love for one another."
John 13: 34-35

Pray Back John 13:34-35

There is no greater love in this world
than the love You have for me Jesus.
Nothing can come close or compare
and all You are asking of me is to
love others with this same love.
In a world of darkness, this can be
very hard, but I need to remember
that You came and lived also in this
world of darkness, and You set an
example and left us Your Word as
a reminder. Help me in my weakness
Lord, to have this love for others
so that they will know, I am Yours.
Amen

"And let us consider how to stir
up one another to love and good
works, not neglecting to meet together,
as is the habit of some, but encouraging
one another, and all the more as you
see the Day drawing near."
Hebrews 10:24-25

Pray back Hebrews 10:24-25
You have told us to meet together
in Your Name Lord and promised
to be with us there. Help us to put aside
our selfish wants when the time comes
to assemble, so that we may give
love and help others and encourage
each other, for the day of Your coming
is near.
Amen

"indeed God considers it just
to repay with affliction those
who afflict you, and to grant
relief to you who are afflicted"
2Thessalonians 1:6-7

Pray Back 2 Thessalonians 1:6-7
You are a good and just God and
You have already provided for those
of us who love You. You are the One
who will pay back those who trouble me
and You will give me relief when I am
troubled. Help me to remember to
leave these things to You Lord, and not
attempt to resolve them myself.
Amen

"for we walk by faith, not by sight"
2 Corinthians 5:7

Pray Back 2 Corinthians 5:7
As a child of Yours Lord,
I am to have faith. I am to believe
that no matter what, You are
taking care of me. I am to believe especially
in what I cannot see. That is true faith,
and most of the time I can do this,
but sometimes doubt slips in, when
things aren't coming together as fast
as I would like or not coming together at all.
This, above all other times, is when I need to
remember who I am and who You are and
banish fear and doubts from my thoughts.
I must trust in You and I do.
Amen

"For the word of the LORD
is upright, and all his work
is done in faithfulness.
He loves righteousness and
justice; the earth is full of the
steadfast love of the LORD."
Psalm 33: 4-5

Pray Back Psalm 33: 4-5
Your Word is truth Lord.
Your Word is upright, and all
You do for us is done in faithfulness
because you love what is good and
right and just. This earth we live in
is full of Your love Lord, and all we
have to do it grab it!
You have put it here for all!
Thank You Lord.
Amen

"Humble yourselves before the Lord,
and he will exalt you."
James 4:10

Pray Back James 4:10

Humility. A hard way to go in this
dog eat dog, me first world we live in.
But as I walk through my day Lord,
show me that I am not most important,
that I do not have to be best or first.
It is only then, when I am on my knees,
when I am on my face, when I am crying
out to You for forgiveness, that
You will lift me up.
Thanking You Father.
Amen

"Likewise the Spirit helps us
in our weakness. For we do not
know what to pray for as we ought,
but the Spirit himself intercedes
for us with groanings too deep
for words."
Romans 8:26

Pray Back Romans 8:26

Thank you Father for sending
Your Holy Spirit to live in me
and help me when I am weak.
Some days prayer eludes me.
Some days words elude me
and I don't know how to
form the words to talk to You.
But the Spirit knows, and in
those moments He is there with me,
interceding with wordless groans
that only You and He understand.
Wordless Words that speak for me.
Amen

"Love is patient and kind; love does not envy or boast; it is not arrogant or rude. It does not insist on its own way; it is not irritable or resentful; it does not rejoice at wrongdoing, but rejoices with the truth. Love bears all things, believes all things, hopes all things, endures all things."
1 Corinthians 13: 4-7

Pray Back 1 Corinthians 13: 4-7
Love is You Father. You are patient and kind. You do not envy or boast nor are you proud. You do not dishonor us Your people nor are You self-seeking. You do not anger as easily as You should and most important, You do not keep track of my wrongs. Father, You do not delight in the evil that is in this world but You always rejoice when truth prevails. Your love is always here to protect, show me trust and give me hope. All of which enables me to persevere through life. Thank You my Father for being love for me.
Amen

"So whatever you wish that
others would do to you,
do also to them, for this
is the Law and the Prophets."
Matthew 7:12

Pray Back Matthew 7:12

In everything I do everyday Lord,
I need to seek you and consider how
I treat others. Do I want to be treated
with disdain, harmed or ridiculed?
No. This is what it all boils down to.
Correct me each time I fail Father.
For it is by Your Word I will
see eternal life.
Amen

"Ask, and it will be given to you;
seek, and you will find; knock,
and it will be opened to you.
For everyone who asks receives,
and the one who seeks finds,
and to the one who knocks
it will be opened.
Matthew 7: 7-8

Pray Back Matthew 7: 7-8
Eternal life with you is there
for me Lord, if only I will ask,
if only I will seek, if only
I will knock. This is the promise
Your Word reveals to me and eternal
life with You in Your Heavenly Kingdom
is all that matters and is all I seek.
Amen

"Count it all joy, my brothers,
when you meet trials of various
kinds, for you know that the
testing of your faith produces
steadfastness."
James 1:2-3

Pray Back James 1:2-3
Your Word says to consider
it pure joy when I face trials.
This is a hard pill to swallow
Lord, this is a very hard thing
to do because the pain gets
in the way. But in my heart, in the
deepest parts of my heart, I know
that this test will make me stronger
for each trial that will come after it,
and there will be more because
of the world I live in. My strength
is in You Lord Jesus
and You alone.
Amen

"Seek good, and not evil,
that you may live; and
so the LORD, the God of
hosts, will be with you,
as you have said.
Hate evil, and love good"
Amos 5:14-15

Pray Back Amos 5:14-15

To seek good and not evil
seems like a reasonable request
Lord, but in this dark world
I am living in, it becomes very hard.
I do hate evil and I do love good.
Help me to look for the good
in all I can and live out the
goodness as best I can for You
are always with me and with
You by my side I have vision
for the good.
Amen

"And we all, with unveiled face, beholding the glory of the Lord, are being transformed into the same image from one degree of glory to another. For this comes from the Lord who is the Spirit."
2 Corinthians 3:18

Pray Back 2 Corinthians 3:18
As I grow to know You better each day Lord, as I grow in Your Word, as I listen more and more to Your Voice, I take on Your glory. What an honor, what a privilege, to shine with Your light more and more each day. Let my light, which is Your Glory, shine in the lives of others.
Amen

"In this is love, not that we have
loved God but that he loved
us and sent his Son to be the
propitiation for our sins"
1 John 4:10

Pray Back 1 John 4:10
When life seems unfair,
when loss comes,
when my heart is broken,
I need only remember God
that You love me so much
that you sent Your Son
who was living in Heaven
with You to this dark and
twisted earth just to die a
sacrificial death and for
one reason only, that I might
live eternally with You.
This is love.
Amen

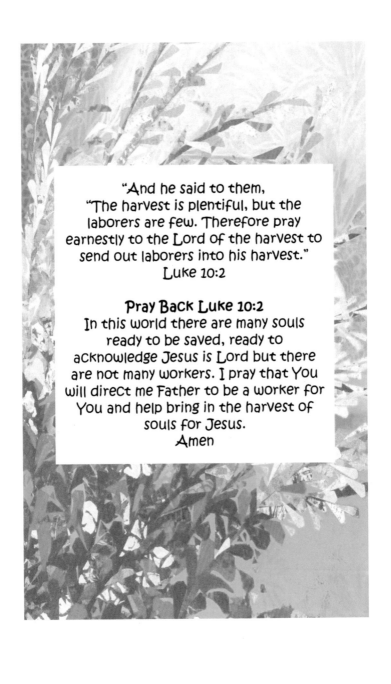

"And he said to them,
"The harvest is plentiful, but the
laborers are few. Therefore pray
earnestly to the Lord of the harvest to
send out laborers into his harvest."
Luke 10:2

Pray Back Luke 10:2
In this world there are many souls
ready to be saved, ready to
acknowledge Jesus is Lord but there
are not many workers. I pray that You
will direct me Father to be a worker for
You and help bring in the harvest of
souls for Jesus.
Amen

"Beloved, if God so loved us,
we also ought to love one another.
No one has ever seen God; if we
love one another, God abides in us
and his love is perfected in us."
1 John 4:11-12

Pray Back 1 John 4:11-12
You who created me loved me
so much and all You require is my
love for others You created.
I've never seen You with my eyes,
Father God, no one has, but with
You living in me and perfecting
Your love in me, then that is how
others see You and I, likewise, see
You in those who have You living
in them. Help me to remember this
when that shadow passes over me
and I am tempted to let it in.
Amen

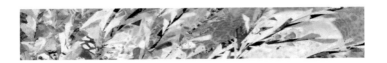

The LORD is my light and
my salvation
whom shall I fear?
The LORD is the
stronghold of my life
of whom shall I be afraid?"
Psalm 27:1

Pray Back Psalm 27:1
Father God,
who do I have to fear?
Of whom shall I be afraid?
With You living in me,
with You as my light and
salvation, with you as the
stronghold of my life,
I have nothing or
no one to fear.
Amen

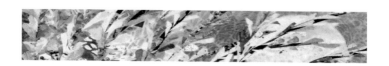

"The steps of a man are
established by the LORD,
when he delights in his way;
though he fall, he shall not
be cast headlong, for the
LORD upholds his hand."
Psalm 37: 23-24

Pray Back Psalm 37: 23-24
I love you Lord and You
make each step I take a
firm one. Sometimes it doesn't
feel firm, sometimes my steps
are wobbly but I know You
are there to hold me up.
Your righteous hand
holds me up.
Thank You Father.
Amen

"The eyes of the LORD
are in every place,
keeping watch on the
evil and the good."
Proverbs 15:3

Pray Back Proverbs 15:3

You are watching me always
Lord, keeping a watchful eye
on my words and my deeds.
I should never feel alone.
And you are watching bad
and good, not just in me
but in everyone.
You are omnipresent.
You are God,
You are "I AM".
Amen

"Trust in the LORD forever,
for the LORD GOD is an
everlasting rock".
Isaiah 26:4

Pray Back Isaiah 26:4
You Lord are my rock.
You are eternal,
You are the One
true God. Forgive me
when I put my trust
in man who is as
mortal as I am and
not who I should
turn toward.
I will trust in You
forever and
You alone.
Amen

"Listen to advice and
accept instruction,
that you may gain wisdom
in the future. Many are the
plans in the mind of a man,
but it is the purpose of the
LORD that will stand."
Proverbs 19:20-21

Pray back Proverbs 19:20-21
I fail here so many times Father.
I sometimes think I don't need
advice or discipline yet that is
what You tell me to do to be
considered wise. I want to do
things my way and history has
shown me that my way is not
the way and Your purpose for
me is what will win in the end.
Teach me Lord.
Amen

"By the word of the LORD
the heavens were made,
and by the breath of his
mouth all their host."
Psalm 33:6

Pray Back Psalm 33:6
You spoke it Father, and
it was made. You breathed
on it and it all appeared.
How glorious and wonderful
You are! What a powerful
and sovereign God You are.
How can anyone look out
over the universe, look at man,
look at nature and
doubt these truths?
Amen

I lift up my eyes to the hills. From where does my help come? My help comes from the Lord, who made heaven and earth. —Psalm 121:1-2

"I lift up my eyes to the hills.
From where does my help come?
My help comes from the LORD,
who made heaven and earth."
Psalm 121:1-2

Pray Back Psalm 121:1-2
I look on this day Lord, and I turn my
eyes toward the world as I seek to
know where my help comes from. But
then Your Spirit speaks to me and I
know that my help doesn't come from
the world, my help comes from You,
the One who made Heaven and Earth
and all that is in it.
Amen

"Give us this day our
daily bread."
Matthew 6:11

Pray Back Matthew 6:11

In the prayer You taught us Jesus,
we ask for our daily bread.
When I pray this it is not just
about food to sustain my body,
but food to sustain my soul
and provision for my daily needs....
not wants....needs. In the morning
I ask You to give me my daily bread,
throughout the day I thank
You when my daily bread is
given and in the evening
I thank You for all these
provisions through the day.
I thank You now Lord.
Amen

"For everything there is
a season, and a time for
every matter under heaven"
Ecclesiastes 3:1

Pray Back Ecclesiastes 3:1
For everything that is in this
life Lord, You have given it a
season and a time and the
ups and downs that go with it.
Of course, I prefer the ups
but I know the downs will come.
Help me to see the good times
as well as the hard for what
they are, a part of life in this
fallen world. But most of all
let me use both to draw
nearer to You,
my Rock and my Salvation.
Amen

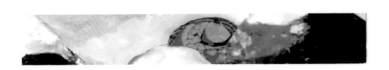

"preach the word;
be ready in season and
out of season; reprove,
rebuke, and exhort,
with complete patience
and teaching."
2 Timothy 4:2

Pray Back 2 Timothy 4:2
I need to be always ready
to tell Your story Lord,
not only when it is the "right"
time but when it is the
"wrong" time also. I want
to tell others of Your great
love for them and tell it
truthfully, not make it up
to be something it is not
and to do so gently
and patiently.
Amen

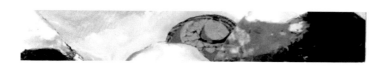

"for at one time you were
darkness, but now you are
light in the Lord.
Walk as children of light"
Ephesians 5:8

Pray Back Ephesians 5:8
There was a time Lord,
when I walked in darkness
even knowing Your light
was there waiting for me,
but thanks be to You God,
I now walk in the light
that is You. Help me every day
to walk in that Light so that
others will see the beauty
of Your love.
Amen

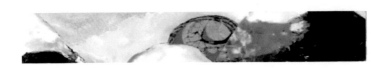

"Worship the LORD
in the splendor of
holiness; tremble before
him, all the earth."
Psalm 96:9

Pray Back Psalm 96:9
I worship You my Father
and my God. I worship Your
holiness, Your splendor,
Your majesty and I do
not forget Your power.
I tremble before You as
all the earth will also.
Amen

"Let not your hearts
be troubled. Believe in
God; believe also in me."
John 14:1

Pray Back John 14:1
Your Words are a comfort
to me Jesus knowing You
have said that if I believe
in God that I can believe
in You also and I do.
Knowing You and knowing
and believing Your Word
soothes my troubled heart.
Amen

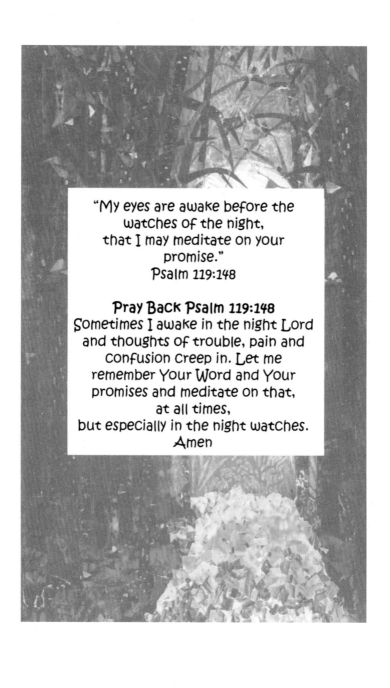

"My eyes are awake before the watches of the night, that I may meditate on your promise."
Psalm 119:148

Pray Back Psalm 119:148
Sometimes I awake in the night Lord and thoughts of trouble, pain and confusion creep in. Let me remember Your Word and Your promises and meditate on that, at all times, but especially in the night watches.
Amen

"In this the love of God was made manifest among us, that God sent his only Son into the world, so that we might live through him."
1 John 4:9

Pray Back 1 John 4:9
What love is this!! What amazing and profound love is this!! You gave me Your only child that through belief in Him, through faith in Him, through trust in Him.... I will live!! Praise be to You Abba Father!
Amen

"When the righteous cry
for help, the LORD hears
and delivers them out of
all their troubles. The LORD
is near to the brokenhearted
and saves the crushed in spirit."
Psalm 34:17-18

Pray Back Psalm 34: 17-18

When I am in distress Lord,
when I am broken, I tend to
feel You are not near.
I tend to feel You have
abandoned me, but all
I need is to turn to Your Word
that says You hear me and
not only that you hear me
but that you deliver me
and are close to me and
indeed, above all else,
have not abandoned me.
Thank You Jesus.
Amen

"for God gave us a spirit
not of fear but of power
and love and self-control.
Therefore do not be ashamed
of the testimony about our Lord."
2 Timothy 1:7-8

Pray Back 2 Timothy 1:7-8
I need to tell others
about You Lord, but
sometimes, when I go to
speak, the words don't come,
fear does. Strengthen me by
Your Word Lord and give
me that spirit of power and
love and self-control so that
I may tell others
of Your great
sacrifice for all.
Amen

"I will give thanks to the
LORD with my whole heart;
I will recount all of your
wonderful deeds.
I will be glad and
exult in you;
I will sing praise
to your name,
O Most High"
Psalm 9:1-2

Pray Back Psalm 9:1-2
I give You thanks my Lord
and my King. I give You
thanks with all of my
heart and soul and I will
remember the things You
have done for me and not
the bad things this world brings.
I lift up my voice and my heart
in praise to Yours Name
Most Holy God.
Amen

"So we do not lose heart.
Though our outer self
is wasting away, our inner
self is being renewed
day by day"
2 Corinthians 4:16

Pray Back 2 Corinthians 4:16
This body You gave to me,
this vessel, is wasting away.
It has been wasting away
since the day I was born,
but what I choose to do
with the inner self is what
matters. My choice is to
daily, throughout my life,
grow and learn for the
betterment of
the inner part
of me, my soul,
and to renew my spirit
by Your Word.
This is my choice.
Amen

"Whoever covers an
offense seeks love,
but he who repeats
a matter separates
close friends."
Proverbs 17:9

Pray Back Proverbs 17:9
To over look the offense
of others toward me is
hard to do Lord, but better
if I want to share love
and be loved. If not,
I will be separated from
people I love because of
an offense that may have
not been that at all.
Help me to discern.
Thank You Jesus for
forgiving my offenses.
Amen

"So I went down to the
potter's house, and there
he was working at his wheel.
And the vessel he was making
of clay was spoiled in the potter's
hand, and he reworked it into
another vessel, as it seemed
good to the potter to do."
Jeremiah 18:3-4

Pray Back Jeremiah 18: 3-4

How broken I am Lord,
a clay vessel, fragile and
spoiled and soiled,
but You pick me up
in Your powerful and
Almighty hand and You
put me on the wheel
and You remake me
into something good.
This is Your grace,
Your unconditional grace.
Thank You Lord.
Amen

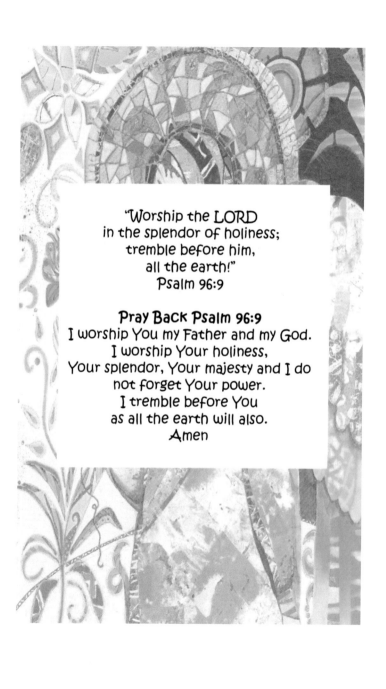

"Worship the LORD
in the splendor of holiness;
tremble before him,
all the earth!"
Psalm 96:9

Pray Back Psalm 96:9
I worship You my Father and my God.
I worship Your holiness,
Your splendor, Your majesty and I do
not forget Your power.
I tremble before You
as all the earth will also.
Amen

"And this is the confidence
that we have toward him,
that if we ask anything
according to his will he hears us.
And if we know that he hears us
in whatever we ask, we know
that we have the requests
that we have asked of him."
1 John 5: 14-15

Pray Back 1 John 5: 14-15
Give me confidence Father
to understand that when
I come to You asking for
anything that is in Your will,
You hear me and if I know
You hear me, I also know
You will give me what
I ask of You.
In Your will...not mine.
Amen

"For the grace of God has appeared,
bringing salvation for all people,
training us to renounce ungodliness
and worldly passions,
and to live self-controlled,
upright, and godly lives
in the present age."
Titus 2:11-12

Praying Back Titus 2:11-12

Thank you God, for Your grace
that offers salvation to me and
to all people. Teach me to say "No"
to ungodliness and the passions
of this world. Teach me to live
a life of self-control, to stand
upright and live a Godly life
in this present age.
Amen

"Trust in the LORD, and do good;
dwell in the land and befriend
faithfulness. Delight yourself
in the LORD, and he will give you
the desires of your heart."
Psalm 37:3-4

Pray back Psalm 37:3-4
I will trust You Lord and
do my best to do good.
My food will be faithfulness.
I will find delight in You Lord
and enjoy Your presence and trust
You to take care of my
desires and needs.
Amen

"For I am sure that neither
death nor life, nor angels
nor rulers, nor things present
nor things to come, nor powers,
nor height nor depth, nor anything
else in all Creation, will be able to
separate us from the love of God
in Christ Jesus our Lord."
Romans 8:38-39

Pray back Romans 8:38-39
Nothing...NOTHING.. nothing....
Can separate me from the love you
have for me in my Lord and Savior
Jesus Christ! Not death or life,
angels or demons, the present or
the future or anything else anywhere
in Creation! I stand convinced Lord
of this truth in all things in my life.
Thank you Father for that love
that is stronger than anything else.
Amen

"For I know the plans I have for you,
declares the LORD, plans for welfare
and not for evil, to give you a future
and a hope."
Jeremiah 29:11

Pray Back Jeremiah 29:11
My Father, I graciously thank You
for being in control of my life.
For reminding me in Your Word that
You have good things planned out for me
and that they are not plans that
will harm me, but plans to prosper me
and most of all give me hope and a future.
You are faithful Lord and I must remember
this in all things.
Thank You.
Amen

"For you, O Lord, are good
and forgiving, abounding in
steadfast love to all who call
upon you.
Psalm 86:5

Pray Back Psalm 86:5
You are the I AM Lord
and you are the One who
forgives my sins and sets me
back on the path and
You are more than good to me.
Your love abounds not just to me
but anyone and all who will call on You.
I pray for all people everywhere
to call on Your Name Lord God,
and receive the gift of Life!
Amen

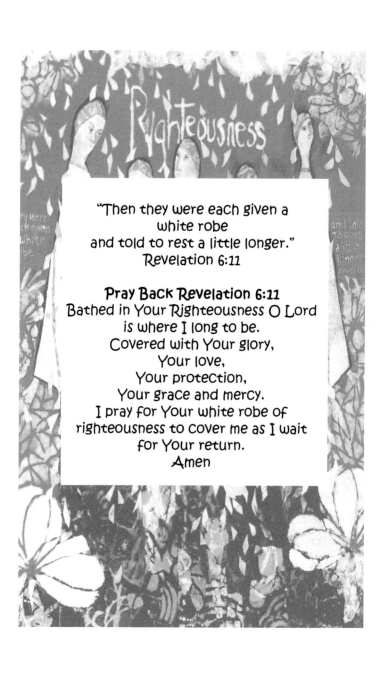

"Then they were each given a
white robe
and told to rest a little longer."
Revelation 6:11

Pray Back Revelation 6:11
Bathed in Your Righteousness O Lord
is where I long to be.
Covered with Your glory,
Your love,
Your protection,
Your grace and mercy.
I pray for Your white robe of
righteousness to cover me as I wait
for Your return.
Amen

"Count it all joy, my brothers,
when you meet trials of various
kinds, for you know that the
testing of your faith produces
steadfastness."
James 1:2-3

Pray Back James 1:2-3
Your Word says to consider it pure joy
when I face trials. This is a hard pill
to swallow Lord, this is a very hard
thing to do because the pain gets
in the way. But in my heart, in the
deepest parts of my heart, I know that
this test will make me stronger for each
trial that will come after it, and there will
be more because of the world I live in.
My strength is in You Lord Jesus
and You alone.
Amen

"but as he who called you
is holy, you also be holy in
all your conduct, since
it is written,
"You shall be holy, for I am holy."
1 Peter 1:15-16

Pray Back 1 Peter 1:15-16

You, O Father, have petitioned
us to be holy as You are Holy.
In this unholy world we live in,
it can be very hard. Give me
strength to seek that holiness daily,
to be "set apart" from the darkness
that is around me and be the light
You have called me to be.
Amen.

"Wash yourselves; make yourselves clean; remove the evil of your deeds from before my eyes; cease to do evil, learn to do good; seek justice, correct oppression; bring justice to the fatherless, plead the widow's cause."
Isaiah 1:16-17

Pray Back Isaiah 1:16-17
You have washed me and made me clean Jesus, by Your death, so why is it I still do things unclean in Your sight? Correct me Lord and show me the path that You would have me take. The path that does right, seeks justice, defends the oppressed, takes up for those without families, those without hope. Take evil out of my sight O' Lord! Amen

"Do all things without grumbling
or disputing, that you may be
blameless and innocent, children
of God without blemish in the midst
of a crooked and twisted generation,
among whom you shine as lights
in the world."
Philippians 2:14-15

Pray Back Philippians 2:14-15
When I find myself grumbling,
complaining, and arguing with others,
remind me that when I turn from
that activity I become blameless
and pure and Your child living
faultless in this corrupt and
crooked generation. What a wonderful
place to be, shining among these
people like a star in the sky.
Amen

And the glory of the LORD
shall be revealed, and all flesh
shall see it together,
for the mouth of the LORD
has spoken."
Isaiah 40:5

Pray Back Isaiah 40:5
Your glory Lord is revealed
everyday for all to see if we will
only open our eyes and our ears.
And one day Your glory will be
revealed for all to see whose eyes
and ears have been closed.
Blessed be Your Name!
Amen

"Brothers, if anyone is caught
in any transgression, you who
are spiritual should restore him
in a spirit of gentleness.
Keep watch on yourself,
lest you too be tempted."
Galatians 6:1

Pray Back Galatians 6:1
It's hard Lord to criticize others
who are sinning without seeming
judgmental or self-righteous,
but it's Your Word and as I read
Your Word with understanding
I can see that it is required to do
so to my brothers and sisters in
Christ and not those outside the faith
and it is to be done gently, not with
a judgmental tone or attitude.
Help me in doing this Father and
help me to proceed with caution
that I too might not be tempted
to fall into their ways.
Amen

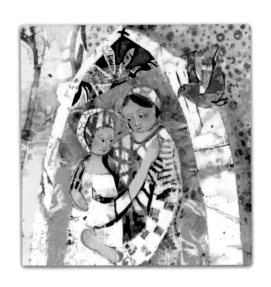

"Therefore a man shall leave
his father and his mother
and hold fast to his wife,
and they shall become
one flesh."
Genesis 2:24

Pray Back Genesis 2:24
Father, how beautiful
You made the relationship
between a man and his wife,
much like the marriage
between Christ and His Church.
Help me to always honor my
husband as You honor me,
as You honor us,
Your Church.
One.
One flesh.
One heart.
One love.
Amen

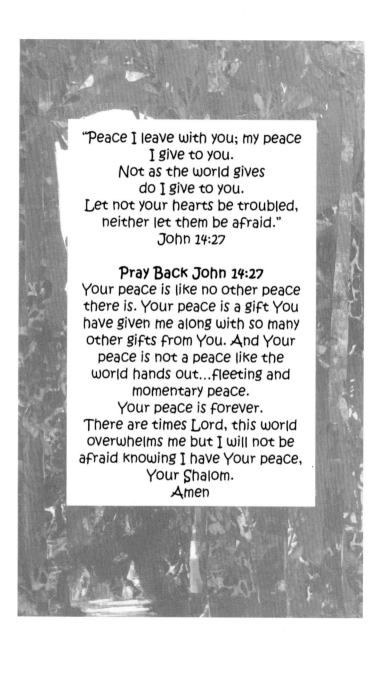

"Peace I leave with you; my peace
I give to you.
Not as the world gives
do I give to you.
Let not your hearts be troubled,
neither let them be afraid."
John 14:27

Pray Back John 14:27

Your peace is like no other peace
there is. Your peace is a gift You
have given me along with so many
other gifts from You. And Your
peace is not a peace like the
world hands out...fleeting and
momentary peace.
Your peace is forever.
There are times Lord, this world
overwhelms me but I will not be
afraid knowing I have Your peace,
Your Shalom.
Amen

"If you abide in my word,
you are truly my disciples,
and you will know the truth,
and the truth will set you free."
John 8:31-32

Pray Back John 8 31-32
It seems so simple, so easy,
to just study Your Words
Jesus, hold to Your teachings,
and do them. It's not that easy
because of all the evil and
temptation in this world,
but I keep working on it each
and every day, being in Your Word
and learning the truth and
knowing that in the truth there is
freedom from this world.
Thank You Jesus.
Amen

"let the wicked forsake
his way, and the unrighteous
man his thoughts;
let him return to the LORD,
that he may have compassion
on him, and to our God,
for he will abundantly pardon."
Isaiah 55:7.

Pray Back Isaiah 55:7

I turn my back on the
ways of my past,
on the unholy thoughts
I've had and deeds I've done.
I turn to You Lord and thank
You for your mercy on me
and for pardon
of all my sins.
Amen

"Do nothing from selfish
ambition or conceit, but
in humility count others
more significant than
yourselves. Let each of
you look not only to his
own interests, but also
to the interests of others."
Philippians 2:3-4

Pray Back Philippians 2: 3-4
I fail on this regularly Lord,
thinking of my own ambition
and self and not valuing
others above myself, not looking
to what they need but just what
I need. Work with me on this
Father, to stop and think
and act in the best interest
of others, as Your Word tells
me to do. Thank You Father
for your patience with me.
Amen

"Therefore, if anyone is in
Christ, he is a new creation.
The old has passed away;
behold, the new has come."
2 Corinthians 5: 17

Pray Back 2 Corinthians 5:17
I am in You Christ!
I am a new creation,
full of You and Your
glory and grace and
mercy and salvation!
That person I used to be
is gone and all that is left
is this new person loving
only You Jesus.
Serving only You!
Amen

"Come to me,
all who labor and
are heavy laden,
and I will give you rest."
Matthew 11:28

Pray Back Matthew 11:28

So many times I have come
to You Holy Father, in physical,
mental and spiritual pain.
So many times I have come
to You tired and worn down
and unable to go on under
my own power. So many times
I have come to You, and
so many times You have
given me rest.
Thank You Father.
Amen

"Therefore, confess your
sins to one another and
pray for one another,
that you may be healed.
The prayer of a righteous
person has great power
as it is working"
James 5:16

Pray Back James 5:16
When I have wronged
You Lord, I confess and
ask for prayer from a
brother or sister in Christ
so that healing will begin.
And I pray in turn for
them so they may be
healed. It's Your Word.
It is what You have instructed
me to do. Prayer has great
power and is my path to You.
Prayer heals. Thank You Lord
for that open pathway
that lays before me
unobstructed.
Amen

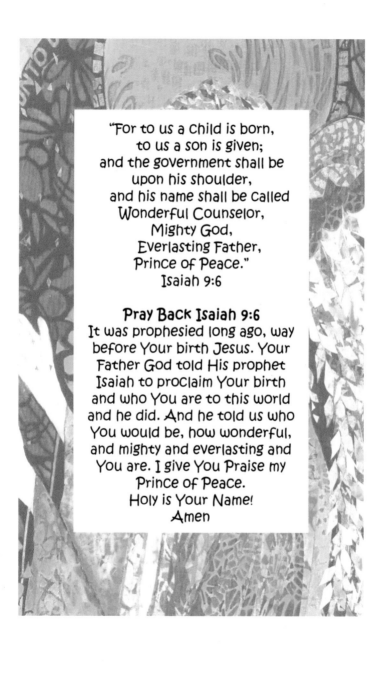

"For to us a child is born,
to us a son is given;
and the government shall be
upon his shoulder,
and his name shall be called
Wonderful Counselor,
Mighty God,
Everlasting Father,
Prince of Peace."
Isaiah 9:6

Pray Back Isaiah 9:6
It was prophesied long ago, way
before Your birth Jesus. Your
Father God told His prophet
Isaiah to proclaim Your birth
and who You are to this world
and he did. And he told us who
You would be, how wonderful,
and mighty and everlasting and
You are. I give You Praise my
Prince of Peace.
Holy is Your Name!
Amen

"Therefore, preparing your minds for action, and being sober-minded, set your hope fully on the grace that will be brought to you at the revelation of Jesus Christ."
1 Peter 1:13

Pray Back 1 Peter 1:13
It is most important Lord
for me to be alert, to study
and know Your Word,
to know Your voice and
not the voice of this world.
My eyes are fixed on the
grace You bring and will
fully bring when Jesus
comes again.
Thank You for
that hope Lord.
Amen

"For the grace of God
has appeared, bringing
salvation for all people,
training us to renounce
ungodliness and worldly
passions, and to live
self-controlled, upright,
and godly lives
in the present age,"
Titus 2:11-12

Pray Back Titus 2:11-12

Your grace is here for
me Lord, all I have to do
is reach out and take it.
Your salvation is here for
me and all mankind. All
I have to do is say "No"
to this world and all its
darkness and live a
self-controlled, upright
and godly life now.
It is a choice and
it is available to all.
Amen

"When you pass through
the waters, I will be with
you; and through the rivers,
they shall not overwhelm
you; when you walk through
fire you shall not be burned,
and the flame shall not consume you."
Isaiah 43:2

Pray Back Isaiah 43:2
When my path is hard,
when life is pushing back
against me, when my world
is turning upside down,
when trouble comes
knocking at my door,
when doubt enters....
You are there Lord.
You are with me,
You keep the darkness
away and give me hope.
Thank You my Father.
Amen

"Bless the LORD, O you his angels,
you mighty ones who do his word,
obeying the voice of his word!
Bless the LORD, all his hosts,
his ministers, who do his will!
Bless the LORD, all his works,
in all places of his dominion.
Bless the LORD, O my soul!"
Psalm 103:20-22

Pray Back Psalm 103:20-22
The angels bless Your Name
O Lord, the mighty ones
who do your bidding,
they obey Your Word as
do all the heavenly hosts
who do Your will.
I praise You O Lord,
for all Your works
everywhere. My soul
praises Your Holy Name.
Amen

"who, though he was in
the form of God, did
not count equality with
God a thing to be grasped,
but emptied himself, by
taking the form of a
servant, being born
in the likeness of men."
Philippians 2: 6-7

Pray Back Philippians 2: 6-7
You, Lord Jesus, left
Your heavenly throne and
came to this earth and
did not regard Yourself
to be equal with God
although You are God,
but You emptied Yourself
and took the form of
common man and became
one of us so that we might
live eternally with You.
What love is this?
What a love this is.
Amen

"She will bear a son,
and you shall call his
name Jesus, for he
will save his people
from their sins."
Matthew 1:21

Pray Back Matthew 1:21
And so it was Father,
You sent Your Son,
Jesus Christ, into
this world and gave
Him the Name Jesus,
and His purpose,
from the beginning
of time, was to bring
us Salvation.
What a precious birth,
what a precious Savior.
Thank You God
for this gift.
Amen

"And while they were going to buy,
the bridegroom came, and
those who were ready went
in with him to the marriage feast,
and the door was shut."
Matthew 25:10

Pray Back Matthew 25:10
Oh Lord, I want to be ready!
I don't want to be unprepared
when it comes time to
go into Your Kingdom.
I don't want to be left behind,
not ready, with my oil lamp unlit.
Help me daily Lord to live for
You and Your Word, so that
I do not miss the
marriage feast.
Amen

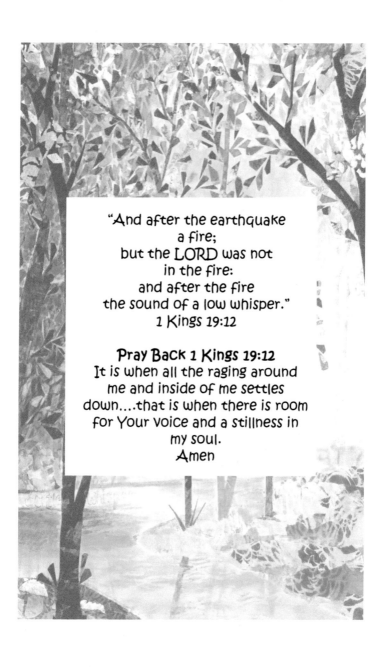

"And after the earthquake
a fire;
but the LORD was not
in the fire:
and after the fire
the sound of a low whisper."
1 Kings 19:12

Pray Back 1 Kings 19:12
It is when all the raging around
me and inside of me settles
down....that is when there is room
for Your voice and a stillness in
my soul.
Amen

"Your kingdom come,
your will be done,
on earth as it is
in heaven."
Matthew 6:10

Pray Back Matthew 6:10
I pray always for Your
Kingdom to come here
on earth Lord. I pray for
that perfect will of Yours
to be done here as it is
done in heaven where You
live. What I need to not
do is presume I know what
Your good and perfect
will is, for myself or for others.
So when I pray, "Thy will be done",
I need to mean it. Your will,
not mine, not what I think
it should be but what
You deem it to be.
This is my prayer.
Amen

"Whoever believes in me,
as the Scripture has said,
'Out of his heart will flow rivers of living
water.'" John 7:38

Pray Back John 7:38
You have said it Jesus,
that following the scripture
and believing in You produces
a heart flowing with living water.
The Holy Spirit who You sent
to live in us if we believe.
I believe. I have that Living Water
flowing in me. Guide me in
showing this to others that
they may have it also.
It is a blessed place to be.
Amen

"But the fruit of the
Spirit is love, joy, peace,
patience, kindness, goodness,
faithfulness, gentleness,
self-control; against such
things there is no law."
Galatians 5:22-23

Pray Back Galatians 5:22-23
Lord, as a believer You
have given me the fruit
of Your spirit. In my
worldliness, the qualities
sometimes get lost. I pray
that when this happens,
Your Holy Spirit will
activate them for me.
Teach me to show kindness
to those who are trying
my patience. Holy Spirit,
I pray that You remove
the abrasive qualities
of my character.
Amen

"Why are you cast down,
O my soul, and why are you
in turmoil within me?
Hope in God; for I shall
again praise him,
my salvation and my God."
Psalms 42:11

Pray Back Psalms 42:11

Some mornings everything
looks bleak. My soul is
disappointed, sad, down.
But why? I have You Lord.
I have Your mercy and I
have hope. What more can
I need or want. When I am
down I need only turn to
You and You show me
the simple joys I overlook
when my mind is not on You.
Thank You for always
reminding me through
Your Word.
Amen

"If you do well, will you not be
accepted? And if you do not do well,
sin is crouching at the door.
Its desire is for you, but you
must rule over it."
Genesis 4:7

Pray Back Genesis 4:7
It is so easy for me Lord,
to be positive and thankful
and appreciative when
life is going good and
I am doing well, but,
I must remember that
satan is ever crouching
at the door just waiting
for me to fail so I will
give into sin and go his way.
This is not my desire.
This is not Your desire.
Give me strength to rule
over sin and accept my
lot and know You
are ever with me.
Amen

"And my God will
supply every need
of yours according
to his riches in glory
in Christ Jesus."
Philippians 4:19

Pray Back Philippians 4:19
Your blessed Word says
You will supply every need
of mine. Need, not want.
Open my heart to this
Lord, when I pray and help
me to recognize need
from want. When I get
to thinking my life is
desperate, that I "must" have,
open my eyes to look around
and realize You have provided
me with all my needs.
Thank You Father.
Amen

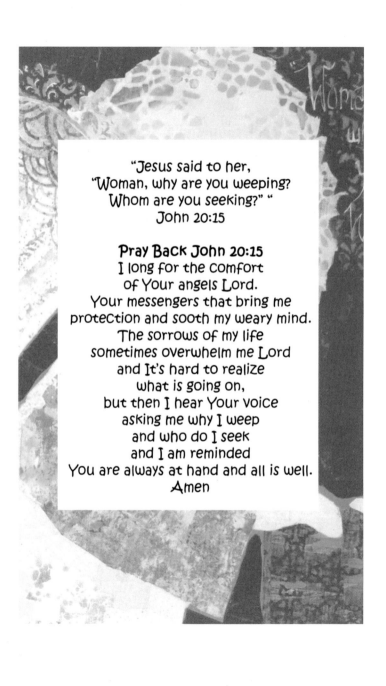

"Jesus said to her,
"Woman, why are you weeping?
Whom are you seeking?" "
John 20:15

Pray Back John 20:15
I long for the comfort
of Your angels Lord.
Your messengers that bring me
protection and sooth my weary mind.
The sorrows of my life
sometimes overwhelm me Lord
and It's hard to realize
what is going on,
but then I hear Your voice
asking me why I weep
and who do I seek
and I am reminded
You are always at hand and all is well.
Amen

"Blessed are those who
mourn, for they shall
be comforted"
Matthew 5:4

Pray Back Matthew 5:4

Grief is a terrible pain Lord,
one that tears up the
heart and soul. But I
have felt Your comfort,
Your hand on me,
Your soothing touch and
I continue to feel it each
and every day. You know
that pain, You know that
grief for you experienced
it when Your Son was
brutally crucified for us
and You know it each time
we grieve. I am thankful
You have pulled me up
and comforted me in my
times of grief and that
You continue to each day.
I love you Father.
Amen

"If then you have been raised with Christ, seek the things that are above, where Christ is, seated at the right hand of God. Set your minds on things that are above, not on things that are on earth."
Colossians 3:1-2

Pray Back Colossians 3: 1-2

This is a reminder I need daily Lord. The reminder that this is not my eternal home and the things here do not matter as much as the things where You are, Jesus, seated at the right hand of Your Father. Help me, when I get too much in this world, to remember to set my mind on things eternal not things that don't last.
Amen

"Let the word of Christ
dwell in you richly, teaching
and admonishing one another
in all wisdom, singing psalms
and hymns and spiritual songs,
with thankfulness in your hearts
to God."
Colossians 3:16

Pray Back Colossians 3:16
How glorious it is Lord
to have your Word dwelling
in me so that not only
will I have Your Word, but
that I will be able to give
it to others through worship,
through hymns and songs
with wisdom and thankfulness
in my heart.
Amen

"The steadfast love of
the LORD never ceases;
his mercies never come
to an end; they are new
every morning;
great is your faithfulness."
Lamentations 3:22-23

Pray Back Lamentations 3:22-23

Your love never ends Father,
Your mercy extends to me
forever. Each new day
brings new mercies,
new hope for my life
and the life of all.
Your faithfulness is
always there even in the
darkest times.
Thank You my Savior.
Amen

"If anyone says, "I love God," and hates
his brother, he is a liar; for he who does
not love his brother whom he has seen
cannot love God whom he has not seen.
And this commandment we have from him:
whoever loves God must also
love his brother."
1 John 4: 20-21

Pray Back 1 John 4: 20-21
Your Word is truth and You
have said it Lord. I am to not
hate my brother and sister,
I am to love them and pray for
them even when they are hard
to love. For me, in my human
condition, this can be hard.
Remind me always to give them
to You in prayer and release them.
How true is Your Word...
how can I say I love You
and hate them. They are made
in Your image just as I am.
Help me Father, to always
remember this.
Amen

"He has told you,
O man, what is good;
and what does the
LORD require of you
but to do justice,
and to love kindness,
and to walk humbly
with your God?"
Micah 6:8

Pray Back Micah 6:8
You have shown me what
is good Lord and You
have shown me what little
You require of me. To be
just and love mercy and
to walk humbly with You.
Help me to open my eyes
and my heart to You.
Amen

"He said to him the third time,
"Simon, son of John, do you
love me?" Peter was grieved
because he said to him the
third time, "Do you love me?"
and he said to him, "Lord,
you know everything;
you know that I love you."
Jesus said to him,
"Feed my sheep.
John 21:17

Pray Back John 21:17

I hear Your call Savior,
I hear You asking me if I love
You, and I hear myself saying
"Yes Lord, You know I
love You", but do I miss
what You say Master?
Do I miss the part about
feeding Your sheep? Or do
I just go about my life
parroting the words,
"You know I love You".
Search me Lord and
heal my selfish heart.
Amen

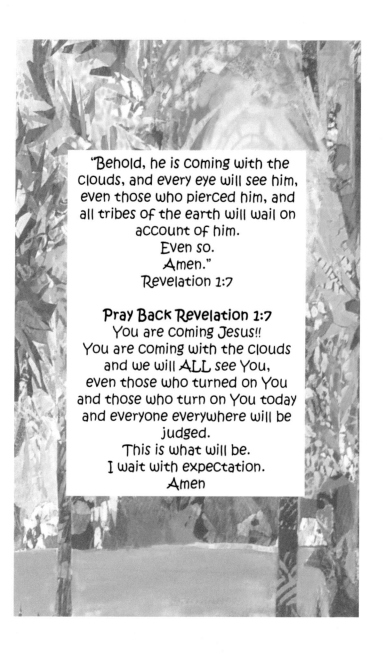

"Behold, he is coming with the clouds, and every eye will see him, even those who pierced him, and all tribes of the earth will wail on account of him.
Even so.
Amen."
Revelation 1:7

Pray Back Revelation 1:7
You are coming Jesus!!
You are coming with the clouds and we will ALL see You,
even those who turned on You and those who turn on You today and everyone everywhere will be judged.
This is what will be.
I wait with expectation.
Amen

"For my thoughts are not
your thoughts, neither are
your ways my ways, declares
the LORD. For as the heavens
are higher than the earth,
so are my ways higher than
your ways and my thoughts
than your thoughts."
Isaiah 55:8-9

Pray Back Isaiah 55: 8-9
What I think and what I do
are not what You think
or what You do Father
and that is as it should be.
Your thoughts and ways
are higher than I can conceive
and Your thoughts and
ways are better.
Let me always
remember this truth.
Amen

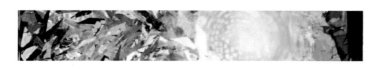

"In my distress
I called to the LORD,
and he answered me."
Psalm 120:1

Pray Back Psalm 120:1
I belong to You Lord.
I have given my life
to You and in times of
heartache, in times of
distress, in times of trouble,
I call to You and You are
always there. You answer
me in ways I sometimes
cannot see or hear or touch,
but You always answer.
You are my Lord.
Amen

"It is the LORD who goes
before you. He will be
with you; he will not
leave you or forsake
you. Do not fear
or be dismayed."
Deuteronomy 31:8

Pray Back Deuteronomy 31:8
You go before me Lord.
You go out ahead of me
and make my path.
Sometimes I get off that
path but when I do
I need not be afraid
or disappointed because
You are always there to
help me Lord to get back on it.
You do not leave me alone,
You do not forsake me.
I love You Lord.
I thank You Lord.
Amen

I cry to you, O LORD;
I say, "You are my refuge,
my portion in the land
of the living."
Psalm 142:5

Pray Back Psalm 142:5
I call out to You Lord
and You only, in the good
times as well as the bad.
There is no other.
You are all I need,
You are my protection,
You are the One who saves
me in the world I must
live in.
Thank You Father
for always being
my refuge.
Amen

"so shall my word be
that goes out from
my mouth; it shall not
return to me empty,
but it shall accomplish
that which I purpose,
and shall succeed in
the thing for which I sent it."
Isaiah 55:11

Pray Back Isaiah 55:11

When I speak Lord the
words leave me and only
return to me with that
accomplishment I intended
it to be and my spoken
words succeed in the
reason I spoke them.
This goes for a bad word
as well as a good.
Oh that You would calm
my tongue Lord, that what
goes out from me is
for good only and will
accomplish only good.
Amen.

"But the path of the righteous
is like the light of dawn which
shines brighter and brighter
until full day."
Proverbs 4:18

Pray Back Proverbs 4:18

You are the Light and Your path
is the way Jesus. One day You
are coming again. Your Word promises
that and as we wait we choose.
I choose Your path and the
brightness it provides more
and more each day as I travel
this life toward You.
Amen

About the Author

Suzi Dennis

Suzi is a self-taught, working artist who works out of her studio at her home in Hot Springs, Arkansas on beautiful Lake Hamilton, which she shares with her husband, 4 cats and 2 dogs. When she began drawing and painting somewhere around age 10, she never dreamed she would someday make her living from her art. "It didn't come overnight and it's nothing I've spent my life working toward", says Suzi. "It was a gradual thing." She spent 25 years of her life working "real" jobs and raising children and it wasn't until she was over forty that the process began for her to be where she is today. Through the years, as her faith and relationship with Jesus Christ grew, her art began to take on the light of her faith and her journaling turned into prayers from her daily scripture readings. Suzi states, "I feel that God gave me this gift and it is my responsibility to give Him all the glory!"

47938319R00091

Made in the USA
Columbia, SC
04 January 2019